79
MAR   Mark, Mandy
J
WITHDRAWN

W9-BWW-948

Extreme Snowmobiling

BLAZERS

TO THE EXTREME

Extreme Snowmobiling

by Mandy R. Marx

3 1389 01831 3817

Reading Consultant:
Barbara J. Fox
Reading Specialist
North Carolina State University

Capstone
press

Mankato, Minnesota

Blazers is published by Capstone Press,
151 Good Counsel Drive, P.O. Box 669, Mankato, Minnesota 56002.
www.capstonepress.com

Copyright © 2006 by Capstone Press. All rights reserved.
No part of this publication may be reproduced in whole or in part,
or stored in a retrieval system, or transmitted in any form or by
any means, electronic, mechanical, photocopying, recording, or otherwise,
without written permission of the publisher.
For information regarding permission, write to Capstone Press,
151 Good Counsel Drive, P.O. Box 669, Dept. R, Mankato, Minnesota 56002.
Printed in the United States of America

Library of Congress Cataloging-in-Publication Data
Marx, Mandy.
    Extreme snowmobiling / by Mandy R. Marx.
    p. cm.—(Blazers. To the extreme)
    Includes bibliographical references and index.
    ISBN-13: 978-0-7368-5465-8 (hardcover)
    ISBN-10: 0-7368-5465-7 (hardcover)
    1. Snowmobiling—Juvenile literature. I. Title. II. Series.
GV856.5.M37 2006
796.94—dc22   2005020090

Summary: Describes the sport of extreme snowmobiling, including
    gear, safety equipment, and competitions.

Editorial Credits
Carrie A. Braulick, editor; Jason Knudson, set designer; Kate Opseth
    and Jennifer Bergstrom, book designers; Wanda Winch, photo
    researcher; Scott Thoms, photo editor

Photo Credits
AutoGraphs Photography/Doug Ogden, 12, 13, 22–23
Corbis/Richard Hamilton Smith, 25
Getty Images Inc./Brian Bahr, 27; Chris McGrath, 20, 21
Red Bull Photofiles/Christian Pondella, 5, 7; Mike Poznansky, 6; R. Van
    Every, cover
Slednecks Inc./John Keegan, 18; John Layshock, 11, 15; Mike Poznansky,
    8; Stella Cooney, 12–13, 17, 28–29

The author dedicates this book to her parents.

The publisher does not endorse products whose logos may appear on
objects in images in this book.

1 2 3 4 5 6 11 10 09 08 07 06

6/07

Table of Contents

Fuel and Fury

The downtown streets are lit up for the Fuel and Fury competition. Without a snowflake in sight, the course seems like an odd place for snowmobiles.

But it is here that snowmobilers test their courage. They do amazing tricks while soaring over 100-foot (30-meter) jumps.

Judges decide which riders did
the best stunts. The winners proudly
show off their trophies.

BLAZER FACT

In 2002, the first Fuel and
Fury competition was held
in Jackson Hole, Wyoming.

Tricks of the Trade

Extreme snowmobiling is all about stunts. Riders practice stunts in hilly country areas. They also test their skills in freestyle competitions.

Rock solid

Hart attack

Tricks include the Hart attack, the rock solid, and the cliffhanger. In the rock solid, the rider doesn't even touch the snowmobile.

The Hart attack is named for motocross freestyle rider Carey Hart. Hart invented the trick.

Cliffhanger

The backflip is one of the hardest stunts. Imagine flipping a machine that weighs 400 pounds (181 kilograms)!

BLAZER FACT

Jay Quinlan performed the first backflip in competition in 2003.

Fully Equipped

Riders call their snowmobiles sleds. The best sleds for freestyle tricks are lightweight and powerful.

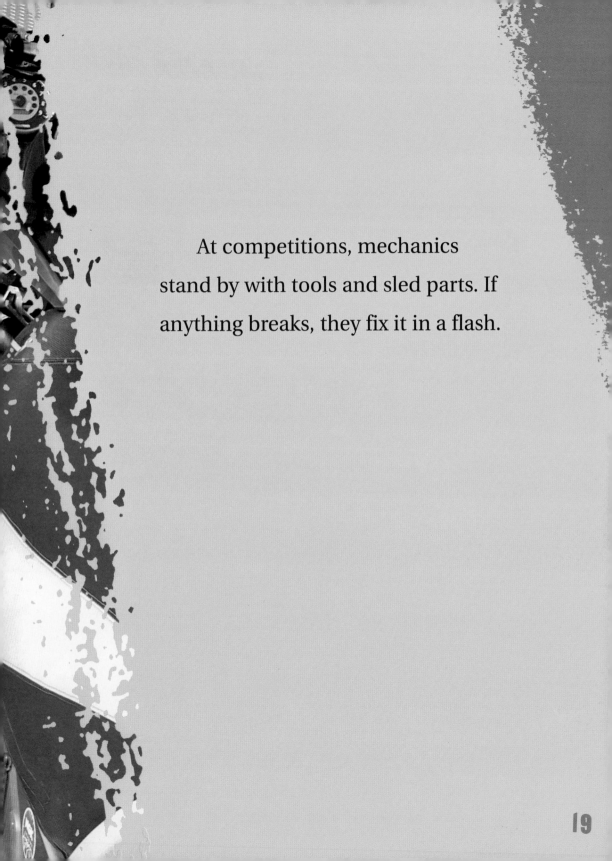

At competitions, mechanics stand by with tools and sled parts. If anything breaks, they fix it in a flash.

BLAZER FACT

In 2005, Jimmy Blaze crashed his sled while trying a backflip.

Crashes can cause serious injuries. Boots, helmets, and body armor all help keep riders safe.

Freestyle Diagram

Track

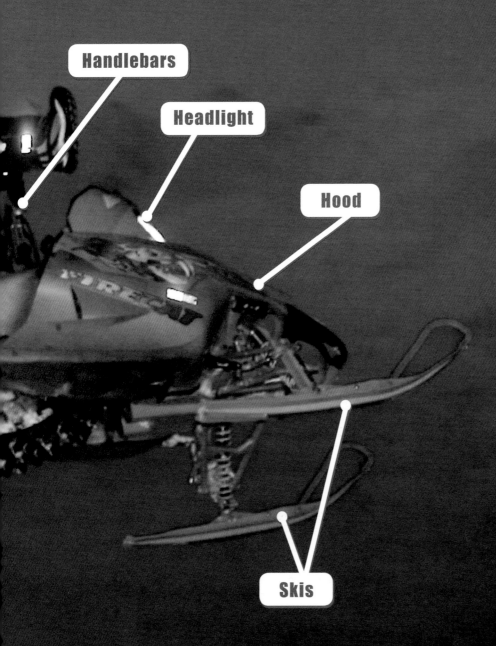

Handlebars

Headlight

Hood

Skis

Riding to Win

Extreme snowmobiling takes courage and practice. Riders learn basic skills before trying tricks.

Riders work hard to make their tricks perfect. They also invent their own tricks, pushing the sport to new limits.

BLAZER FACT

Riders submit videos of their riding to qualify for competitions.

A Hart attack in action!

Glossary

body armor (BOD-ee AR-mur)—a plastic shield with foam lining that freestyle snowmobilers wear to protect their chests

course (KORSS)—a track or area where a competition is held

freestyle (FREE-stile)—an extreme snowmobiling style that includes jumps and tricks; riders perform their tricks at freestyle competitions.

helmet (HEL-mit)—a hard hat that protects the head

mechanic (muh-KAN-ik)—someone who fixes vehicles or machinery

Read More

Budd, E. S. *Snowmobiles.* Sport Machines at Work. Chanhassen, Minn.: Child's World, 2004.

Clemson, Wendy. *Using Math to Conquer Extreme Sports.* Mathworks! Milwaukee: Gareth Stevens, 2005.

Maurer, Tracy Nelson. *Snocross.* Radsports Guides. Vero Beach, Fla.: Rourke, 2003.

Internet Sites

FactHound offers a safe, fun way to find Internet sites related to this book. All of the sites on FactHound have been researched by our staff.

Here's how:

1. Visit *www.facthound.com*
2. Type in this special code **0736854657** for age-appropriate sites. Or enter a search word related to this book for a more general search.
3. Click on the **Fetch It** button.

FactHound will fetch the best sites for you!

Index